D0577615

CRABS & MOLLUSKS

Brenda Ralph Lewis

Northern Plains Public Library
Ault Colorado

GARETH**STEVENS**

GS

PUBLISHING
A Member of the WRC Media Family of Companies

Please visit our web site at: **www.garethstevens.com**
For a free color catalog describing Gareth Stevens Publishing's
list of high-quality books and multimedia programs,
call 1-800-542-2595 (USA) or 1-800-387-3178 (Canada).
Gareth Stevens Publishing's fax: (414) 332-3567.

Library of Congress Cataloging-in-Publication Data

Lewis, Brenda Ralph.
    Crabs & mollusks / Brenda Ralph Lewis. — North American ed.
        p. cm. — (Nature's monsters: Water creatures)
    Includes bibliographical references and index.
    ISBN 0-8368-6176-0 (lib. bdg.)
    1. Crabs—Juvenile literature. 2. Mollusks—Juvenile literature.
    I. Title: Crabs and mollusks. II. Title. III. Series.
    QL444.M33L47   2006
    595.3'86—dc22   2005054176

This North American edition first published in 2006 by
Gareth Stevens Publishing
A Member of the WRC Media Family of Companies
330 West Olive Street, Suite 100
Milwaukee, WI 53212 USA

Original edition and illustrations copyright © 2006 by International Masters Publishers AB.
Produced by Amber Books Ltd., Bradley's Close, 74–77 White Lion Street, London N1 9PF, U.K.

Project editor: Michael Spilling
Design: Joe Conneally

Gareth Stevens editorial direction: Valerie J. Weber
Gareth Stevens art direction: Tammy West
Gareth Stevens production: Jessica Morris

All rights reserved. No part of this book may be reproduced, stored in a retrieval system,
or transmitted in any form or by any means, electronic, mechanical, photocopying, recording,
or otherwise, without the prior written permission of the copyright holder.

Printed in the United States of America

1 2 3 4 5 6 7 8 9 10 09 08 07 06

Contents

Continents of the World

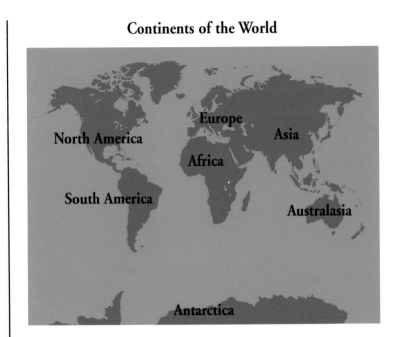

North America

Europe

Asia

Africa

South America

Australasia

Antarctica

The world is divided into seven continents — North America, South America, Europe, Africa, Asia, Australasia, and Antarctica. In this book, the area where each animal lives is shown in blue, while all land is shown in green.

Words that appear in the glossary are printed in **boldface** type the first time they occur in the text.

Giant Squid

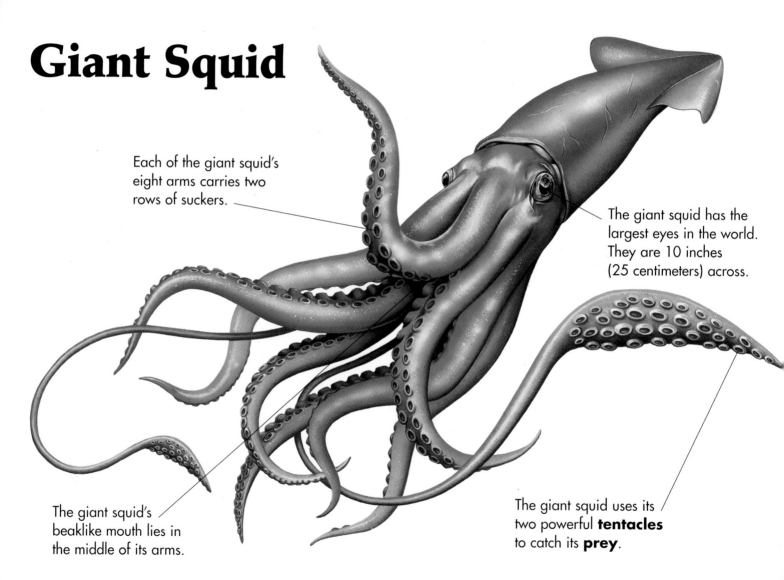

Each of the giant squid's eight arms carries two rows of suckers.

The giant squid has the largest eyes in the world. They are 10 inches (25 centimeters) across.

The giant squid's beaklike mouth lies in the middle of its arms.

The giant squid uses its two powerful **tentacles** to catch its **prey**.

Giant squids are so huge that only one other sea creature dares to attack them — the sperm whale. Whales face great danger, however, when catching squids for food.

Size

Did You Know?

Giant squids are mysterious creatures. Although many people have looked, no one has found their **habitat**, or home, in the depths of the ocean.

2 Whales that have survived battles with giant squids have been found with terrible injuries on their bodies. The squid's mighty suckers have sharp, razorlike edges. They leave deep round marks and cuts on their prey.

1 The giant squid has many weapons for fighting a sperm whale. Its arms are very strong and have a powerful grip. Its bony beak is sharp and can cause a lot of damage to a sperm whale's hide.

Where in the World

Three species of giant squid have been found, all of them in the world's deepest oceans, including the Pacific, Atlantic, and Indian Oceans and the cold North Sea.

Giant Octopus

The octopus can lie at any angle, but its eyes remain level.

The giant octopus is the largest octopus in the world. It can grow up to 23 feet (7 meters) long.

Cells on its skin hold sacs of color. The octopus moves these sacs to change its colors.

Each of the eight tentacles of the giant octopus has 280 suckers.

The giant octopus was behind many old stories of sea adventures. These tales described great monsters that dragged whole ships down to the bottom of the ocean.

Size

Did You Know?

The giant octopus can break down a prey's hard shell in three different ways. It pulls the shell apart, it bites it open, or it "drills" through the shell by softening the surface with its **saliva** and scraping a hole.

1 The diver is much smaller than the giant octopus. The octopus has wrapped one tentacle around the diver's leg, but it may just be curious.

2 The giant octopus is very intelligent and learns a lot by touching. Its suckers have special taste and touch **sensors** that send messages to its brain. Once it realizes the diver is not a threat, it may let him go.

Where in the World

The Pacific species of giant octopus lives along the Californian coast, the Aleutian Islands, and Japan. Two other species live off the South American and southern African coasts.

7

Blue-Ringed Octopus

The octopus, normally brown, shows its blue rings before attacking its prey.

Like all octopuses, the blue-ringed octopus has eight tentacles, or "legs."

The poison in two large **glands** kills the octopus's prey in minutes.

With its powerful, beak-shaped mouth, the octopus eats its food very quickly.

8

The soft-bodied, slow-moving blue-ringed octopus is very small — about the same size as a golf ball. It may seem easy prey to other sea creatures. They often discover their mistake.

Size

Did You Know?

A single bite from a blue-ringed octopus contains enough poison to kill twenty-six people. The bite is painless but quickly paralyzes the victim. The prey dies soon afterwards.

1/ Looking for food, a blue-ringed octopus has left the hole in the reef where it lives. A coral trout passes close by. It does not notice the blue-ringed octopus.

3/ The octopus hits back and pierces the coral trout's head with its beak. The trout is doomed. Quickly **paralyzed**, it drifts helplessly away and will soon die.

2/ The octopus starts flashing its blue rings. The fish does not understand the warning signal. Not realizing the danger, it moves to attack the octopus.

Where in the World

There are two types of blue-ringed octopus. The first lives in reefs and pools off the southeastern Australian coast. The second, more deadly, animal lives near islands in the Indian and Pacific Oceans.

Northern Plains Public Library
Ault Colorado

Spider Crab

The spider crab's long **pincers** can pick up tiny pieces of food.

The crab's eight legs look just like the legs of a spider.

Tiny plants and animals attached to its shell **camouflage** the spider crab.

Spider crabs have creamy white bodies underneath their reddish brown or gray shells.

Spider crabs that grow to immense sizes, such as the Japanese spider crab, have been called sea monsters. Long ago, seamen on sailing ships told scary tales about them.

Size

Did You Know?

The giant Japanese spider crab is one of the world's largest **crustaceans**. Measured from side to side from the tip of one leg to another, it can reach 13 feet (4 m) across.

1 Giant crabs live in the depths of the ocean, where the **pressure** is very high. The giant spider crabs live on the seabed itself. Their shells are very hard and tough, so they do not break apart because of the pressure.

2 Giant spider crabs seem to be all legs. Their legs are so long that they could step over an automobile without touching it.

Where in the World

Spider crabs live in all the seas and oceans on Earth. Many live in shallow **coastal** waters, where they can find plenty of food.

11

Opalescent Squid

Squids signal each other by using special **luminescent** cells in their skins.

Suckers on the opalescent squid's tentacles hold tightly to its food.

Opalescent (oe-puh-LEH-sunt) squids have enormous eyes, covered with a **transparent membrane** for protection.

Two of the squid's tentacles grab its prey, while another eight pull it into the squid's mouth.

Opalescent squid are one of the most deadly hunters in the oceans. Once a squid has a hold on its prey, the animal has no chance of escape. The squid is too quick and too powerful.

Size

Opalescent squid can make themselves nearly invisible when they are hunting for food, so their prey cannot see them. They do this by changing the color cells in their skin to match their background.

1 The opalescent squid moves at high speed by blasting out a powerful jet of water from behind. This blast forces it forward so fast that the fish is taken by surprise.

2 When it is close enough, the squid shoots out one of its long feeding tentacles and grabs its prey. Soon, more of the tentacles wrap around the fish. The fish may struggle hard. It will not survive, however, once the squid uses its beak to inject it with paralyzing poison.

Where in the World

These squids live in the Pacific Ocean along the western coast of North America. They prefer the waters off California and Central America, where there is lots of food for them to hunt and eat.

13

Horseshoe Crab

The horseshoe crab's shell completely protects its soft body parts.

The horseshoe crab has five pairs of legs, with feet like pincers.

The mouth of the horseshoe crab is found at the center of its legs.

By pointing its tail forward, the crab digs out a path through the sand.

14

At one time, horseshoe crabs were known as "horsefoot crabs" because their round, curved shells look like a horse's hoof. They have lived on Earth for at least 250 million years.

Horseshoe crabs can swim upside down using their ten legs to push themselves along. Their two hundred gills, which are hidden underneath a flap, also help them to move through the water.

Copper in the horseshoe crab's blood makes its blood blue.

2 One reason horseshoe crabs have survived for millions of years is their shells. **Predators** wanting to eat these crabs found it difficult to turn them over, so they could not get at the crabs' soft underbellies. Horseshoe crabs also have four eyes, allowing them to see in every direction at the same time.

1 The back part of the crab's shell covers its gill plates. As well as helping the crab move, the **gills** take **oxygen** from the water so that it can breathe.

Where in the World

Horseshoe crabs live in only two areas of the world. Three species are found in the coastal waters of Asia, while another lives along the Atlantic coast of North America.

Ghost Crab

Ghost crab eyes flip upward, so the crab is able to look in all directions.

This crab hides itself by crouching low in the sand, making it hard to see.

Strong pincers help ghost crabs to tear apart hard-shelled lobsters for food.

Ghost crabs can spend hours out of water, using a special **breathing apparatus** in their body.

Ghost crabs walk along beaches at night, looking for food. They are omnivorous, which means they will eat almost anything. Their food includes clams, lobsters, insects, plants, and even trash.

Did You Know?

When a ghost crab is in danger, it scuttles off so fast that it can travel 65 feet (20 m) within ten seconds. It does this while running sideways!

1 A ghost crab sorts through bits and pieces lying around on the beach. It is looking for tasty tidbits. There is, however, a special treat waiting.

3 The jellyfish has a mighty sting, but the ghost crab is not worried. It tears up the Portuguese man-of-war with its powerful pincers, then mashes it up using its strong jaws.

2 The crab's eyes flip up to look around the beach. A mass of jelly lies on the sand. It is a jellyfish called a Portuguese man-of-war.

Where in the World

Ghost crabs live in tide pools, on beaches, or in mud in the **tropical** parts of the world. These lie in the southern half of the globe, around or below the **equator**.

Northern Plains Public Library
Ault Colorado

17

Sea Slug

The sea slug's featherlike gills take oxygen from the water to breathe.

The **sensory** "horns" on its head help the sea slug find food.

The soft-bodied sea slug has been called a snail without a shell.

Its skin tastes so bad that attackers spit the sea slug out.

Sea slugs have their own uses for the stinging cells of animals they eat as food. They use these cells to attack other creatures or to defend themselves from attack.

Size

Did You Know?

Some sea slugs are called "Spanish dancers." As they move through the water, the soft frills along the length of their bodies sway like dancers' skirts.

2 This hungry starfish thinks the sea slug will make a good meal. The hydroid's stinging cells have moved through the sea slug to the tips of the two tubes standing up on its back. The tubes give the starfish a sharp sting and drive it away.

1 The pink and red sea slug eats a **feathery hydroid**. The hydroid's many stinging cells can paralyze and kill.

Where in the World

Most sea slugs inhabit shallow waters around the edges of the Atlantic, Pacific, and Indian Oceans. Some float along on the deep ocean surface, living off tiny **plankton**.

Hermit Crab

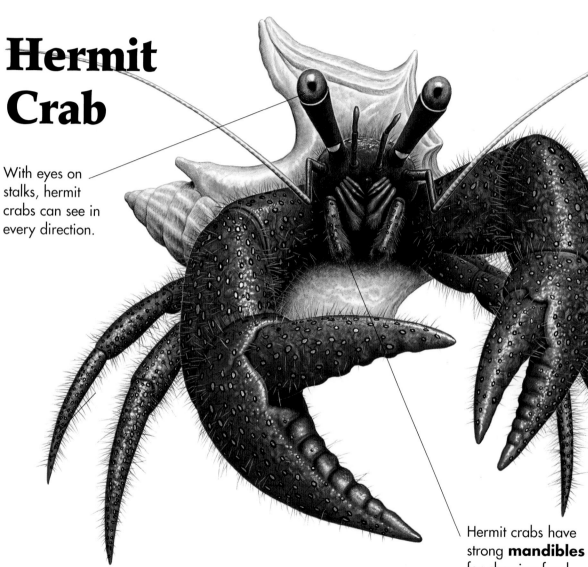

With eyes on stalks, hermit crabs can see in every direction.

The crabs use their long **antennae** to find food and new shells.

These pincers have two purposes — to tear up food and to fight enemies.

Hermit crabs have strong **mandibles** for chewing food.

Hermit crabs do not grow their own shells. They have to find one and move into it. This task is not always easy because other hermit crabs are busy doing the same thing.

Many hermit crabs are kept as pets. As the pet crabs grow, the owners have to buy extra shells that are one-third bigger than the hermit crab.

1 If hermit crabs cannot find a shell to live in, they will not grow to their full size. Once the crab has found a new shell, however, it may have to fight its owner to get it.

2 As the loser in the battle crawls away, a fish watches it hungrily. A hermit crab without a shell is in danger. Its soft body offers no protection, which makes it easier for other creatures to attack and eat it.

Where in the World

Hermit crabs live in every sea and ocean in the world. They usually live on the ocean floor, but some also live in rock pools along coasts and beaches.

Spiny Lobster

Each leg has one claw for gripping the sand or rock.

The spiny lobster uses its flat, paddle-shaped tail to propel itself backward.

Spiny lobsters have three different mouths parts for grabbing, biting, and crunching food.

The spiny lobster's five pairs of legs have **joints** that can bend.

Spiny lobsters will eat other spiny lobsters if they get the chance. If spiny lobsters smell blood, they will follow the scent trail in search of food.

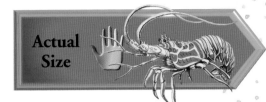

Actual Size

Did You Know?

Spiny lobsters can weigh up to 26 pounds (11.8 kilograms) and can be more than 3 feet (91 cm) long.

Some spiny lobsters live to be more than fifty years old. Octopuses, large fishes, and especially people prey upon spiny lobsters for food.

1 A blood trail leads the lobster to the place where another spiny lobster is lying helpless on its back. It has been in a fight with a big fish that has bitten off most of its legs.

2 The first lobster soon begins tearing up the dying lobster. Using its mouth parts, it rips up the flesh and pushes small pieces into its mouth. Before long, the injured lobster dies. All that remains when the meal is finished is its empty shell.

Where in the World

Spiny lobsters live in the coastal waters of oceans across the world — in the western and eastern Atlantic, the northern and southern Pacific, the Indian Ocean, and the South China Sea.

Cuttlefish

The cuttlefish's frilly fins make gentle ripples as it swims along.

Using **pigments** underneath their skin, cuttlefish can change color rapidly.

Cuttlefish squirt poison from glands inside their mouths to kill their prey.

Cuttlefish shoot out a jet of "ink" to escape from danger quickly.

Cuttlefish are very clever at hiding themselves while waiting for possible food. Their prey cannot easily see them before it is too late. Cuttlefish move too fast for their prey to escape.

Size

Did You Know?

Artists once used cuttlefish ink in paintings. The color of the ink was called sepia, which is a kind of darkish brown.

1 Looking for food, the fish do not notice the cuttlefish hiding among the seaweed. The tentacles of the cuttlefish look like seaweed floating in the water.

2 One fish swims past the seaweed unaware, and the cuttlefish grabs it with its tentacles.

The cuttlefish shoots poison from its mouth into the fish. The fish soon dies, and the 3 cuttlefish has a meal to eat.

Where in the World

There are more than one hundred **species** of cuttlefish. They live all over the world, in sand on the seabed, in coral reefs, on the sides of undersea cliffs, and in seaweed clumps.

Northern Plains Public Library
Ault Colorado

25

Slipper Lobster

Slipper lobsters are unusual because they have a **dorsal** brain.

The slipper lobster's knobbly, spotted, and ridged shell provides camouflage for hiding among rocks.

With their flattened bodies, slipper lobsters can easily slip through narrow cracks.

Slipper lobsters use the big plates on their heads for shoveling sand.

Slipper lobsters will eat carcasses, or the dead bodies, of sea creatures. If two lobsters want the same carcass, however, they will not share it. Instead, they fight for it.

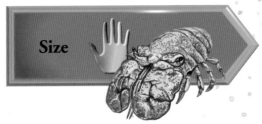

Slipper lobsters are **nocturnal**. They crawl on the seabed at night. When in danger, they escape by moving backward. They flip their tails very quickly to gain speed.

1 Slipper lobsters pick out their own special **territory** on the seabed. These two lobsters have found a dead fish on the border between their territories. Both want the food. Each of them grips it, and they start a tug-of-war.

2 The two lobsters pull so hard that they tear the dead fish in two. The two parts are not equal, however, so one lobster gets most of the fish.

Where in the World

Slipper lobsters live in many environments in the warm coastal waters of the world. They live on muddy, sandy, or rocky sea bottoms or on coral reefs and sea-grass beds.

27

Arrow Crab

Arrow crabs use their spearlike **rostrum** to stab and hold their prey.

The arrow crab's sharp, pointed head lies at the base of its rostrum.

Arrow crabs possess eight **barbed** legs nearly 3 inches (7.6 cm) long.

Their striped bodies make arrow crabs hard to see on **coral reefs**.

Arrow crabs are among the thousands of animals found on coral reefs off the North and South American coasts — on rocks, in sand, or among pieces of broken coral on the seabed.

Actual Size

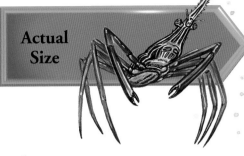

Did You Know?

Arrow crabs are nocturnal creatures, which means they move around at night. They do not mind divers taking photographs of them but will attack any sea creature that enters their territory.

1 Arrow crabs move amazingly fast. Before this young fish knows what is happening, the crab has swooped in and stabbed it through the body with its razor-sharp rostrum.

This arrow crab has made a cage of its legs. The fish is trapped inside it. The crab uses its sharp pincers to carve the fish into tiny pieces. Arrow crabs need to break their food up like this because they cannot eat large chunks. Their bodies **2** are only about 1 inch (3 cm) long.

Where in the World

Arrow crabs live off the coasts of North and South America and on coral reefs between North Carolina and the coast of Brazil, as well as in the South Pacific and Indian Oceans.

Glossary

antennae — long, thin feelers on the heads of crustaceans or insects

barbed — with spikes

breathing apparatus — parts of the body that allow a water animal to breathe on land

camouflage — to disguise or hide something

cells — the smallest parts of a living thing. Cells are the building blocks of all life forms.

coastal — along a coast where the land meets the sea

coral reefs — coral ridges, lying above the surface of the sea, made from the skeletons of sea animals

crustaceans — animals with hard shells that live in water

dorsal — located on the back

equator — a line drawn on maps to mark the center of the hot, tropical belt found around the middle of Earth's surface

feathery — light, like a feather

gills — parts of an animal used for breathing in water

glands — parts of the body that make special chemicals needed for the body to work properly

habitat — place where an animal usually lives

hydroid — a sea animal with no backbone

joints — places where two bones fit together

luminescent — shining with light

mandibles — lower jaws

membrane — thin covering

nocturnal — awake and active at night

opalescent — showing many small points of moving color

oxygen — gas that makes up one-fifth of the air and is also present in water. Animals need oxygen to live.

paralyzed — unable to move

pigments — natural coloring matter in animals or plants

pincers — the limbs of a crab used for grabbing

plankton — tiny sea plants and animals used as food

predators — animals that hunt other animals for food

pressure — the weight of the water in a sea or ocean, especially in the deepest parts

prey — an animal hunted for food

rostrum — a body part shaped like a beak at the front of some animals' heads

saliva — sticky liquid that animals make in their mouths

sensors — parts of an animal that detect sounds, smell, taste, movement, or touch

sensory — able to feel or sense

species — a group of living things of the same family or type

tentacles — long, sensitive feelers used to touch and grab

territory — land that an animal claims as its own

transparent — see-through

tropical — referring to warm regions of the world with lush plant life and lots of rain

For More Information

Books

Crabs and Crustaceans. Looking at Minibeasts (series). Sally Morgan (Thameside Press)

Extraordinary Horseshoe Crabs. Julie Dunlap (Carolrhoda Books)

Hermit Crabs. Lola M. Schaefer (Heinemann-Raintree)

Mollusks and Crustaceans. Science around Us (series). Peter Murray (Child's World)

Mollusks: Snails, Clams and their Relatives. Invertebrates (series). Beth Blaxland (Chelsea House Publications)

The Crab. Kris Hirschmann (KidHaven Press)

Web Sites

Crabs
www.kidskonnect.com/Crabs/CrabsHome.html

Invertebrates for Kids
www.cbel.com/invertebrates_for_kids

Hermit Crab Student Page
projects.edtech.sandi.net/sessions/hermitcrab/ hermitcrab.html

Man and Mollusk
www.manandmollusc.net/kid_zone.html

Marine Life
teachers.westport.k12.ct.us/resource/marine_life.htm

Mollusks
www.mcwdn.org/Animals/Mollusks.html

Index